MW01612823

Electric Smoker Cookbook

50+ Delicious Techniques for Smoked Meat and Fish - 2021 Edition

Henry Bacon

scenarios in which the publisher or the original author of this work can be in any fashion deemed liable for any hardship or damages that may befall them after undertaking information described herein.

Additionally, the information in the following pages is intended only for informational purposes and should thus be thought of as universal. As befitting its nature, it is presented without assurance regarding its prolonged validity or interim quality. Trademarks that are mentioned are done without written consent and can in no way be considered an endorsement from the trademark holder.

Description of Electric Smoker Cookbook

Authoritative smoked taste for those who don't prefer to waste hours monitoring their slow and low barbecue.

With this Electric Smoker Cookbook, you can confidently smoke just about anything, proposing many advantages over traditional and conventional smoking techniques.

Irresistible Recipes: In this book, you will discover irresistible recipes. Each recipe contains an informative and complete method, nutritional facts, cook time, and all the ingredients you need to make a perfect dish.

A complete guide of Electric Smoker: Not only this, but you will also get detailed information about Electric Smoker. Benefits of electric smoker, safety tips, working of an electric smoker, tips for cooking a perfect dish in an electric smoker, maintenance tips, recipes that can be cooked in a smoker, tips for cleaning the electric smoker, and more in the book's introduction.

Table of content

Poultry

1. Smoked Beer-Can Chicken

Ingredients

- 1 whole chicken, 4 to 5 pounds
- 1/2 can of beer barbecue Rub
- 1 tablespoon smoked paprika
- 2 tablespoons brown sugar
- 2 teaspoons salt
- 1 tablespoon chili powder
- 2 teaspoons garlic powder
- 1 teaspoon black pepper-

Beer Barbecue Sauce

- 1 cup ketchup
- 2/3 cup apple cider vinegar
- 3/4 cup beer.
- 1/2 cup brown sugar
- 1/4 cup molasses
- 2 teaspoons onion powder
- 2 teaspoons Worcestershire sauce
- Salt and pepper to taste

Preparation

Prep time: 10 mins, Grilling: 1:15 - 1:30

1. Eliminate and scrap of the neck, giblets, and any extra fat from the chicken. Sprinkle the salt over the whole surface and inside the cavity of the chicken. Enfold the chicken and refrigerate for 1½ to 2 hours.

2. In a small bowl, combine all ingredients in a bowl and blend it.
3. Wash the chicken inside and outside with cold water. pat the chicken dry with paper towels. Apply the rub on each side on the chicken. Fold the wing tips behind the chicken's back.
4. Heat the grill for indirect cooking over medium heat (350° to 450°F).
5. Open the beer can and spill out about half the beer. Using a church key, make two more holes in the top of the can. Place the beer can on a solid surface and plunk the chicken cavity.
6. Add the wood chips to the smoker box of a gas grill, and close the lid. When the wood begins to smoke, transfer the chicken-on-a-can to the grill. Grill over indirect medium heat
7. Using forceps, hold the bird and slide a sturdy, wide spatula under the beer can. Carefully transfer it in an upright position to a plate and serve after 5 minutes.

Nutrition Facts

Amounts Per Serving

- Total Fat: 20g. Saturated Fat: 5g.
- Cholesterol: 235mg.
- Sodium: 230mg.
- Protein: 77g.

2. Herb-Smoked Quail

Ingredients

- 1 teaspoon Dijon mustard
- 1 package quail (Semi-Boneless)
- 1 lemon juice
- 1/4 cup olive oil
- 3 tablespoons herbs (chopped fresh mixed, we used tarragon, chives, thyme, and chervil)
- kosher salt
- Freshly ground black pepper
- Nutritional Guidelines

Preparation

Prep time 1 hour

1. Semi-boneless quail mild, and cook in under 20 minutes. give them a quick marinade in fresh summer herbs, tart lemon, and just a little of Dijon.
2. Pat quail dry with paper towels. In a bowl, blend together Dijon, lemon juice, lemon zest, and olive oil. Stir in herbs. Add quail, turning to coat in the mixture. Enclose and set aside for about 15 minutes. Bring chicken out of the fridge about 20 minutes before grilling.
3. Preheat a lightly oiled grill to medium-high. Place the quail on the grill breast side down. Grill for about 3 minutes then carefully turn over and continue to grill until chicken is just cooked through, about 3-4 minutes more. Cut to a platter to rest for just 5 minutes. Serve it.

Nutrition Facts

- Calories: 192
- Total Fat: 12.05g
- Saturated Fat: 3.38g
- Polyunsaturated Fat: 2.98g
- Monounsaturated Fat: 4.18g
- Cholesterol: 76mg
- Sodium: 53mg
- Protein: 19.63g

3. Crispy-Skin Orange Chicken

Ingredients

- 3 skin-on bone-in chicken breast halves
- Kosher salt and freshly ground black pepper
- 1 tablespoon vegetable oil
- 1/2 cup frozen orange juice concentrate
- 4 tablespoons honey

Preparation

Total: 40 min

1. Preheat the smoker to 375 degrees F.
2. Generously salt and pepper the chicken breast halves. Heat the oil in a large saute pan over medium-high heat and brown the chicken, skin side only, until beginning to crisp, about 5 minutes.
3. Meanwhile, make the orange glaze In a small saucepan, heat the orange juice concentrate, honey, salt and pepper to taste, over medium heat, and boil for 3 minutes. Then remove from the heat.
4. Turn the chicken over and brush each piece with the glaze. transfer the chicken to the smoker. Bake until the internal temperature reaches 160 to 170 degrees F, brushing on more glaze halfway through, about 15 minutes in total. Let the chicken rest for 10 minutes. Remove the chicken breast from the bone and slice the meat on the bias. Transfer the chicken to a serving tray.

Nutrition facts

- Calories 400
- Total Fat 21g
- Cholesterol 55mg
- Sodium 700mg
- Carbohydrates 42g
- Net carbs 41g
- Glucose 24g
- Protein 15g

4. Buffalo Chicken Balls

Ingredients:

- 1 pound ground chicken
- 1 stalk celery, minced
- 2 cups whole wheat bread crumbs
- 1 egg
- ¼ cup melted butter
- ⅓ cup hot pepper sauce
- Salt and ground black pepper to taste
- Cooking spray

Preparation:

Total: 1 hr 55 mins

1. Mix ground chicken, bread crumbs, celery, and egg in a bowl. Melt butter in a saucepan over low heat; stir in hot sauce. Pour into chicken mixture; blend until well absorbed. Add salt and pepper. Cover and refrigerate for 1 hour.
2. Preheat the smoker to 230 degrees C. Spray a large baking dish with cooking spray. Roll chicken mixture into 1-inch balls and place a baking dish. Chicken mixture is quite soft so resting the mixture first will make rolling easier.
3. Bake chicken balls in the preheated smoker until no longer pink in the center, about 30 minutes. An instant-read thermometer installed into the center should read at least 74 degrees C. Remove chicken balls from the smoker and rest for 5 minutes before serving.

Nutrition facts:

- 159 calories
- Protein 13.6g
- Carbohydrates 11.5g
- Fat 6.8g
- Cholesterol 57.1mg
- Sodium 412.9mg.

5. Garlic-Herb Turkey Legs

Ingredients:

- ¼ cup kosher salt
- ¼ cup turbinado sugar
- ¼ cup fresh thyme leaves
- ¼ cup fresh rosemary leaves
- 3 bay leaves
- 2 garlic cloves
- 6 (1- to 1 1/2-lb.) turkey legs
- ¾ cup reduced-sodium chicken broth

Preparation:

Total: 3 hrs 30 mins

1. Add the first 6 ingredients in a food processor for 40 to 45 seconds or until finely chopped. Put turkey legs in a 13- x 9-inch baking dish, and rub with salt mixture. Cover and cold for 12 to 15 hours.
2. Preheat the oven to 400°. Shift turkey to a roasting pan, cutting any accumulated liquid. Flow broth over turkey; let stand 30 minutes. Bake for 1 hour.
3. Decrease temperature to 350°. Cook with pan juices, and bake 1 hour and 30 minutes to 1 hour 45 min or until meat stretches away from the bone, turning legs every 20 minutes. Let hold for 10 minutes before serving.

Nutrition facts:

- Total carbs: 2.9 grams

- Fiber: 1.1 grams
- Sugars: 0.3 grams
- Saturated fat: 17.9 grams
- Sodium: 834 mg
- Magnesium: 49 mg
- Potassium: 452 mg

6. Chipotle Wings

Ingredients

- 4 lb chicken wing and drumette (2 kg)
- ¼ cup cornstarch (30 g)
- 2 teaspoons salt, divided
- 1 teaspoon garlic powder
- 1 ½ cups chipotle peppers in adobo (300 g)
- ¼ cup lime juice (60 mL)
- ¼ cup honey (85 g)

Preparation

Prep time: 1 hr 20 min

1. Pat dry chicken and place in a large mixing bowl or plastic bag. Roll with cornstarch, garlic powder, and one teaspoon of kosher salt.
2. Set the chicken in a single layer on a cookie sheet and freeze for at least an hour, up to overnight.
3. In a food blender, mix chipotles, lime juice, honey, and the remaining salt. Puree until smoot Preparation
4. Pat dry chicken and place in a large mixing bowl or plastic bag. Bob with cornstarch, garlic powder, and one teaspoon of kosher salt.
5. Put the chicken in a single layer on a cookie sheet or wire rack and chill for at least an hour.
6. In a food blender, merge chipotles, lime juice, honey, and the remaining salt. Puree until smooth. Set aside until ready to grill.
7. Preheat the grill to medium-high heat. Grill wings until just starting to brown on the underside, about 5 minutes, then flip and repeat.

8. Using a basting brush, cover the top side of the wings with chipotle puree. Flip and heat until the exterior just start to char. Season the other side, flip and repeat.
9. Transfer wings from heat to a platter and let cool for at least 5 minutes. Serve!

Nutrition facts

- Calories 518
- Fat 35g
- Carbs 17g
- Sugar 12g
- Protein 34g

7. Drunken Drumsticks

Ingredients

- 8-12 chicken legs
- Beer brine (recipe below)
- Jeff's Texas style rub
- Jeff's Barbecue sauce

Preparation:

Cook Time: 1 to 1.5 hours

1. Fill a large container or bowl with 40 ounces (1 quart + 1 cup) cold water.
2. Add two 12-0z glasses of beer
3. Stir in ½ cup of kosher salt and continue to stir until salt is reduced into the water and the water becomes clear.
4. Stir in ½ cup brown sugar making sure it is melted into the water.

Brine the Chicken Drumsticks

1. Combine the drumsticks to a lidded container for bringing.
2. Remove any large clumps of fat or extra skin with a kitchen sharp knife.
3. Once all of the chicken is in the container, pour the brine over the chicken to cover.
4. Close with the lid, and place the brining chicken into the fridge for 3 hours.
5. At the end of the brining time, drop the liquid brine and rinse each piece of chicken to remove any residual salt.

Smoke the Drumsticks

1. Set up your smoker for cooking at 275-300°F with indirect heat.
2. Hold the smoke going for the entire time for great flavor.
3. Use a quick read thermometer to check the temperature after about one-hour.

Nutrition facts:

- Calories 803
- Total Fat15.00g
- Cholesterol 33 mg
- Dietary Fiber 2.0g
- Protein50.00g

8. Sweet Sriracha Barbecue Chicken

Ingredients

- 2.5 lbs. Just BARE Chicken Thighs
- 3 Tablespoons unsalted butter
- 1 Tablespoon minced fresh ginger
- 2 garlic cloves, minced
- 1/4 teaspoon smoked paprika
- 1/4 teaspoon ground cloves
- 4 Tablespoons honey
- 6 Tablespoons Sriracha
- 1 Tablespoon lime juice

Preparation

Prep time: 45 min

1. Heat the smoker to medium-high heat, about 400 °F.
2. In a small saucepan, add butter. Once melted add in fresh ginger and garlic. Stir until aromatic, about 1 minute.
3. Next add in smoked paprika, ground cloves, honey, Sriracha, and lime juice. Stir to mix and let boil for 4-5 minutes.
4. Pat chicken legs dry. Season with salt and pepper on both sides.
5. Splash grill grates with cooking spray.
6. Put chicken thighs on the grill, skin side below first. Grill for 4-5 minutes. Flip the chicken over and grill on the other side for 4-5 minutes.

7. Continue to cook chicken, flipping every 3-4 minutes so it doesn't burn until the internal temperature is 165ºF.
8. During the last 5 minutes of grilling brush the glaze on both sides of the chicken.
9. Transfer from the grill.

Nutrition

- Calories: 477
- Sugar: 21 g
- Sodium: 477 mg
- Fat: 23 g
- Saturated Fat: 9 g
- Carbohydrates: 32 g
- Protein: 35 g
- Cholesterol: 182 mg

9. Applewood Smoked Turkey Breast

Ingredients

- 6-pound boneless turkey breast adjust cooking time depending on weight
- Water Smoker or Charcoal Grill
- A bag of Apple Wood Chips soaked in water
- Charcoal
- Water
- Tongs
- Meat Thermometer Our breast came with a built-in pop-up timer.

Turkey Rub:

- ¼ cup brown sugar packed
- 2 tablespoons chili powder
- 2 tablespoons paprika
- 1 tablespoon cumin
- ½ teaspoon cayenne pepper
- 1 tablespoon garlic powder
- 3 teaspoons mustard powder
- 2 teaspoons salt
- 2 teaspoons black pepper

Preparation

Total Time: 5 hours 30 minutes

1. Rub the turkey prior to it going on the smoker. You could even do it 24-hours earlier. To do this, simply rinse the turkey well and pat dry. Combine rub ingredients together, making sure to break them down into clumps of brown sugar. Blend all the ingredients for the rub in a small bowl and stir to mix. Let it keep in the fridge for at least 4-hours.
2. Set up your smoker. To do this, fill the charcoal bed with unlit fuels and add only a few lit coals to the very top. Preheat the grill to 250 degrees F. To manage this low temperature, use only half as much charcoal as usual.
3. When the smoker is in the ideal temperature range, place the turkey breast on the hot grill over the drip pan, throw a hand full of the soaked wood chips and some dry wood chips onto the coals, and close the grill.
4. Check the temperature of the grill every hour, keeping as close to 250 degrees F as possible. Resist the temptation to open the lid. Only open the charcoal door or the lid if you need to add more charcoal or wet wood chips to maintain temperature and smoke.
5. Smoke the turkey breast until an outside crust forms and the internal temperature of the meat is about 170 to 180 degrees F, about 5 hours.
6. Leaving the turkey to rest before slicing or serving it lets the meat fibers relax, moisture that was driven out is redistributed. A good 15 to 20 minutes rest should do under loosely tented foil.

7. To cut the turkey, lift the pop-up indicator. Slice the breast upon the grain into ½-inch slices. Perfectly roasted meat should be moist and juicy.

Nutrition

- Calories: 517kcal
- Carbohydrates: 13g
- Protein: 98g
- Fat: 8g
- Cholesterol: 244mg
- Calcium: 98mg
- Iron: 4.3mg

10. Jamaican Jerk Chicken

Ingredients:

- 1 medium onion, coarsely chopped
- 3 medium scallions, chopped
- 2 Scotch bonnet chiles, chopped
- 2 garlic cloves, chopped
- 1 tablespoon five-spice powder
- 1 tablespoon allspice berries, coarsely ground
- 1 tablespoon coarsely ground pepper
- 1 teaspoon dried thyme, crumbled
- 1 teaspoon freshly grated nutmeg
- 1 teaspoon salt
- 1/2 cup soy sauce
- 1 tablespoon vegetable oil
- Two 3 1/2- to 4-pound chickens, quartered
- Directions

Preparation:

Total time: 9 hrs

1. In a food processor, mix the onion, scallions, chiles, garlic, five-spice powder, allspice, pepper, thyme, nutmeg, and salt; process to a coarse paste. With the machine on, add the soy sauce and oil in a constant stream.
2. Drain the marinade into a large dish, add the chicken and turn to coat. Wrap and refrigerate overnight. Bring the chicken to room temperature before proceeding.
3. Heat the smoker. Grill the chicken over a medium-hot fire, turning occasionally, until well browned and cooked through 35 to 40 minutes.

4. Transfer the chicken to a platter and serve.

Nutrition facts:

- Calories 185
- Total Fat 12g
- Saturated Fat 2.5g
- Cholesterol 49mg
- Sodium 403mg
- Potassium 186mg

11. Cinnamon-Cured Fire-Smoked Chicken

Ingredients

- 4 cups water
- 1/4 cup coarse salt
- 1/4 cup (packed) dark brown sugar
- 4 skinless boneless chicken breast halves (1 1/2 pounds total)
- 1 small onion, thinly sliced
- 2 thin lemon slices
- 2 cinnamon sticks, broken in half
- 2 cups wood chips (preferably cherry or apple), soaked 1 hour in water to cover, drained
- Cherry Barbecue Sauce

Preparation

Prep time: 1 hr

1. Flutter 4 cups of water, coarse salt, and sugar in a large bowl until sugar dissolves.
2. Combine chicken breasts, sliced onion, lemon slices, and broken cinnamon sticks.
3. Cover the bowl with a plastic cover and refrigerate for 1 hour.
4. Prepare a smoker (medium-high heat). Place wood chips in an 8x6-inch foil packet left open at the top; set the packet atop coals 5 minutes before grilling chicken. Remove chicken from marinade; cut marinade. Grill chicken until just cooked through, about 8 minutes per side. Shift chicken to a plate. Serve, passing Cherry Barbecue Sauce separately.

Nutrition facts:

- Carbs; 1 g
- Dietary Fiber; 0 g
- Sugar; 0 g
- Fat; 0 g
- Saturated; 0 g
- Polyunsaturated; 0 g
- Monounsaturated; 0 g
- Trans; 0 g
- Protein; 12 g
- Sodium; 0 mg
- Potassium; 0 mg
- Cholesterol; 0 m

12. Smoky Brined Turkey

Ingredients

- 2 gallons water
- 1 ½ cups canning salt
- 3 tablespoons minced garlic
- 1 tablespoon ground black pepper
- ¼ cup Worcestershire sauce
- ⅓ cup brown sugar

Preparation

1. Prep time:28 hr 20 min; Servings: 12, Yield: 12 Servings
2. In a food-grade large bucket, large enough to hold your turkey, combine together the water, salt, garlic, pepper, Worcestershire sauce, and brown sugar.
3. Put in a refrigerator, and soak turkey for 2 days before smoking or roasting.

Tips

Always brine foods in a food-grade, nonreactive containers such as stainless steel or enameled stockpot. Never use ordinary trash bags, or metal buckets, or containers not meant for food use.

Nutrition Facts

- 32 calories;
- Protein 0.2g;
- Carbohydrates 8.1g;
- Fat 0g;
- Cholesterol 0mg;
- Sodium 13913.4mg.

13. Caramelized Honey Buffalo Chicken

Ingredients:

- 3 pounds chicken wings or drumettes
- Kosher salt and freshly ground black pepper, to taste
- 1 1/2 tablespoons baking powder
- 1/2 cup tomato sauce
- 1/3 cup hot sauce, such as Cholula
- 1/4 cup honey
- 2 tablespoons unsalted butter
- 2 teaspoons Worcestershire sauce
- 1/2 teaspoon onion powder
- 1/2 teaspoon garlic powder

For the ranch dipping sauce:

- 1/2 cup sour cream
- 1/4 cup buttermilk
- 2 tablespoons mayonnaise
- 1/3 cup chopped fresh chives
- 2 tablespoons chopped fresh dill
- 1/4 teaspoon onion powder
- 1/4 teaspoon garlic powder
- Kosher salt and freshly ground black pepper

Preparation

Prep time: 1 hr 25 min

1. To make the Ranch dipping sauce, mix together sour cream, buttermilk, mayonnaise, chives, dill, onion powder, and garlic powder in a medium bowl; season with salt and pepper, to taste.
2. Preheat the smoker to 425 degrees F. Coat a wire rack with nonstick spray and put on a baking sheet lined with aluminum foil.
3. Using paper towels, pat wings dry. In a large bowl, combine wings, 1 1/2 teaspoons salt, 1 teaspoon pepper, and baking powder.
4. Set wings onto the prepared baking sheet and grill for 40-45 minutes, using metal tongs to turn at halftime.
5. In a small saucepan over medium-low heat, combine tomato sauce, hot sauce, honey, butter, Worcestershire, onion powder, and garlic powder. Bring to a boil; reduce temperature and simmer, stir until slightly thickened, about 15-20 minutes.
6. In a large bowl, add wings and half the tomato sauce mixture. Place wings onto the prepared baking sheet and grill, turning once, until bright and gently caramelized, about 5-7 minutes. Stir in remaining tomato sauce mixture. Serve!

Nutrition Facts:

- Calories 2490
- Total Fat 140g

- Cholesterol 425mg
- Carbohydrates 181g
- Protein 119g

14. Plum Chicken Pops

Ingredients:

- 12 chicken drumsticks
- 2 tsp salt
- 2 tsp pepper

For the plum sauce:

- ¾ of a 16 oz jar of plum jam
- 2 Tbsp apple cider vinegar
- 1 Tbsp brown sugar
- 1 Tbsp minced onion
- 1 tsp crushed red pepper flakes
- 1 clove garlic, minced
- ½ tsp ground ginger
- Salt & pepper to taste

Preparation

Prep time: 55 min

1. First of all, make the plum sauce. Mix all ingredients in a medium saucepan and shift from heat after reaching a boil. Set aside.
2. cut the skin down to the bone just over the bottom end leg joint. Pull skin as much as possible on drumsticks and using needle-nose pliers, remove the thin, white tendons from each leg. You'll need to grasp the meaty end
3. Remove and pluck the long tendons. Grasp the meaty end to help keep more meat in the process.

4. Sprinkle each with salt and pepper and head to the smoker.
5. Use cherry wood and smoke on a Char-broil Electric Smoker for 90 minutes at a constant 250 degrees F.

Nutrition Facts:

- Calories: 313
- Carbs: 18g
- Fat: 6g
- Protein: 40

15. Mesquite Maple-Bacon Chicken

Ingredients

- 5 to 6 skinless boneless chicken breasts
- Salt and pepper
- ¼ cup vegetable oil
- ¾ cup cooked and crumbled bacon
- 1 Tablespoon butter
- 2 Tablespoon garlic
- ½ cup brown sugar
- ¼ cup maple syrup
- 1 Tablespoon yellow mustard

Preparation:

Prep time: 45 to 55 minutes

1. Beat the chicken until it is justly flat and there are not any thicker portions.
2. Salt and pepper the chicken.
3. Heat a large skillet to medium-high temperature and oil. Put the chicken in a skillet and cook on each side for about 5 minutes. Check that there is no longer any pink in the core to make sure it is cooked through and cook longer if needed to reach the proper temperature.
4. Transfer chicken from skillet.
5. Wipe skillet to remove any residue.
6. Over medium high heat, dissolve butter.
7. Add garlic and fry for 30 seconds.
8. Combine brown sugar, maple syrup, mustard, and bacon. Bring to a boil and reduce temperature to low and simmer for 3 minutes until sugar is dissolved.

9. Add chicken back in and spoon sauce over chicken and cook for another 2 minutes. Serve.

Nutrition Facts:

For Serving of 1 piece

- Calories 570
- Total Fat 30g
- Saturated fat 11g
- Monounsaturated fat 10g
- Polyunsaturated fat 7g
- Cholesterol 80mg
- Sodium 1110mg
- Potassium 320mg
- Carbohydrates 49g

16. Smoked Chicken Breasts

Ingredients:

Brine:

- 4 cups water
- ¼ cup kosher salt
- 2 tablespoons brown sugar
- 1 tablespoon cider vinegar
- 4 pounds skin-on, bone-in chicken breasts
- maple wood chips

Dry Rub:

- 1 teaspoon salt
- 1 teaspoon ground black pepper
- 1 teaspoon paprika
- 1 tablespoon brown sugar
- ½ teaspoon garlic powder
- ½ teaspoon onion powder

Preparation:

5 mins Cook: 4 hrs Additional: 4 hrs Total: 8 hrs 5 mins
Servings: 3 Yield: 3 servings

1. Add water, kosher salt, brown sugar, and apple cider vinegar in a large bowl. Stir until salt and brown sugar are dissolved. Put chicken breasts into brine, seal, and refrigerate for at least 4 hours or overnight.
2. Preheat an electric smoker according to 225 degrees F (110 degrees C) using maple wood chips.
3. Transfer chicken breasts from brine and wash under cold water. Pat dry. Mix salt, black pepper,

paprika, brown sugar, garlic powder, and onion powder in a bowl. Spray dry rub all over chicken breasts and place skin-side up on a grill rack in the preheated smoker. Place a drip pan underneath.

4. Smoke chicken breasts in the preheated smoker until chicken is no longer pink at the bone and the juices fall clear, about 4 hours, adding maple wood chips as necessary to keep the smoke continuous. An instant-read thermometer inserted near the bone should read 165 degrees F (74 degrees C).

Nutrition facts:

- 729 calories;
- Protein 126.2g;
- Carbohydrates 14.9g;
- Fat 14.6g;
- Cholesterol 344.8mg;
- Sodium 8680.6mg.

17. Kristina's Atomic Wings Dry-Rub Style

Ingredients:

- 1 tablespoon ground cayenne pepper
- 1 tablespoon ground jalapeño pepper
- 1 tablespoon ground habanero pepper
- ½ teaspoon dried oregano
- ½ teaspoon salt
- ⅛ teaspoon white sugar
- ⅛ teaspoon ground black pepper
- ⅛ teaspoon ground cinnamon
- 12 chicken wings, thawed if frozen

Preparation:

Prep:10 mins Cook:15 mins Total:25 mins Servings:6 Yield:1 dozen chicken wings

1. Mix cayenne pepper, jalapeño pepper, habanero pepper, oregano, salt, sugar, black pepper, and cinnamon in a small bowl; mix well to make dry rub.
2. Put chicken wings in a large resealable bag or container. Add dry rub mixture to wings; seal the container and shake well until evenly distributed.
3. Preheat the smoker for medium heat and lightly oil the grate.
4. Cook the chicken wings on the preheated grill, turning occasionally, until the chicken is well-browned and no longer pink, 15 to 20 minutes.

Nutrition Facts:

- 141 calories

- Protein 12.6g
- Carbohydrates 1.9g
- Fat 9.2g
- Cholesterol 38.6mg
- Sodium 234.5mg

18. Smoked Chicken Rub

Ingredients:

- ¾ cup dark brown sugar
- ½ cup coarse kosher salt
- ½ cup ground espresso beans
- 2 tablespoons freshly ground black pepper
- 2 tablespoons garlic powder
- 1 tablespoon ground cumin
- 1 tablespoon cayenne pepper

Preparation:

Prep: 5 mins Total: 5 mins Servings:10 Yield: 10 servings

1. Mix brown sugar, salt, espresso, black pepper, garlic powder, cumin, and cayenne together in a bowl.

Nutrition facts:

- 78 calories;
- Protein 0.7g;
- Carbohydrates 19.3g;
- Fat 0.3g;
- Sodium 4563.7mg.

19. Kick ass smoked chicken thighs

Ingredients:

- 8 chicken thighs
- Brine
- BBQ Sauce of your choice
- Brine Recipe
- BBQ Rub
- Fruitwood- apple, cherry, etc
- Hickory wood

BRINE RECIPE:

- 1-gallon warm water
- ¾ cup kosher salt
- 2/3 cup sugar
- ¾ cup soy sauce
- ¼ cup olive oil

BEFORE GRILLING DIRECTIONS

Mix your brine ingredients in a large container and let your thighs sit in the brine for 4 hours in the refrigerator or longer before putting on the smoker.

Preparation:

Time: 1 hr 35 mins

1. Oil your grill grates with canola oil so your chicken won't adhere to the grates.
2. Prepare a smoker and indirect grilling with the direct side getting hot enough to sear the chicken briefly.
3. Pat the chicken dry after separating it from the brine. Now, sprinkle your thighs generously with BBQ rub.
4. With the lid off, cook the chicken thighs quickly on the direct side- just until you start to get some coloration.
5. Now, lightly put the thighs on the indirect side. Add wood to the coals. Reduce the grill temperature down to 250 degrees.
6. The chicken should smoke for 45-50 minutes or until the internal temp reads 165 degrees with an internal read thermometer. During the last 5 minutes, apply a coat of your favorite bbq sauce with a brush and it will create a nice golden glaze while on the grill in the last 5 minutes.
7. Once you've reached the proper internal temperature of 165 degrees, take the chicken off the grill and let it rest tented under foil for 10 minutes. serve!

Nutrition facts:

- Calories 160

- Calories from Fat 63 (39.4%)
- Total Fat 7g
- Saturated fat 2g
- Cholesterol 60mg
- Sodium 720mg
- Carbohydrates 4g
- Net carbs 3g
- Sugar 2g
- Fiber 1g
- Protein 19g

20. Sweet and spicy bacon wrapped chicken

Ingredients:

- 1 1/2 pounds boneless skinless chicken thighs*
- 6-8 slices of bacon
- 1 tablespoon chili powder
- 1 teaspoon paprika
- ½ teaspoon garlic powder
- salt and pepper
- 1/2 cup brown sugar
- optional garnish: chopped parsley

Preparation:

Prep Time: 10 minutes, Cook time: 30 min, total time:40 minutes

1. Preheat the smoker to 400 degrees. Mix chili powder, paprika, and garlic powder in a bowl. Twist each chicken piece into the spices and wrap it in bacon. Place in a 10-inch skillet or a 9x13 inch baking dish. Spray the tops with brown sugar.
2. smoke for 30-35 minutes or until the chicken reads 165 degrees and is no longer pink. broil the tops of the chicken for 1-2 minutes to crisp the bacon at the end.

Nutrition facts:

- Calories 453 Kcal
- Carbohydrates 29g
- Protein 37g
- Fat20g
- Saturated Fat6g
- Cholesterol 183 Mg
- Sodium 411mg
- Potassium 569 Mg
- Fiber 1g
- Sugar27g
- Vitamin A880IU
- Calcium 45mg
- Iron 2mg

21. Smoked Steelhead Trout (Salmon)

Ingredients:

- 2 pounds steelhead trout fillets
- 2 tablespoons olive oil
- 4 cloves garlic, chopped
- 1 ½ tablespoon dried rosemary, crushed
- 1 cup sugar-based curing mixture (such as Morton® Tender Quick®)
- 1-quart water
- ground black pepper to taste
- 1 pound alder wood chips, soaked in water or wine

Preparation:

10 mins Cook:5 hrs Additional:8 hrs 30 mins Total:13 hrs 40 mins Servings: Yield:6 servings

1. Wash the fish fillets and place them in a shallow glass baking dish. Drizzle olive oil over the fish and season with garlic and rosemary. Spread the seasonings into the fish. Cover and refrigerate overnight.
2. Dissolve the curing salt in the water and pour it into the dish with the fish. Let it marinate for 15 minutes per half-inch of thickness.
3. Meanwhile, prepare your smoker for a four-hour slow burn using charcoal. The temperature should be at 150 degrees F (65 degrees C) before you get started.
4. Transfer the fish from the brine and discard leftover liquid. Put each piece of fish onto a small

piece of aluminum foil - just big enough to hold the fillet, and season with pepper to taste. Place them on the rack in the smoker. Sprinkle a handful of the soaked wood chips over the coals or place them in a heat box. Cover and allow fish to smoke for 2 hours, adding more wood chips as needed.

5. Increase the temperature in the smoker (add more charcoal) to 200 degrees F and let the fish smoke until the internal temperature of the fillets reaches 165 degrees F. Remove from the smoker and let stay for 20 minutes before serving.

Nutrition Facts:

- 203 calories
- Protein 25.5g
- Carbohydrates 1.3g
- Fat 10.1g
- Cholesterol 125.6mg
- Sodium 18955.6mg

22. Honey Smoked Turkey

Ingredients:

- 1 (12 pound) turkey
- 1 (12 pound) whole turkey
- 2 tablespoons chopped fresh sage
- 2 tablespoons ground black pepper
- 2 tablespoons celery salt
- 2 tablespoons chopped fresh basil
- 2 tablespoons vegetable oil
- 1 (12 ounces) jar honey
- ½ pound mesquite wood chips

Preparation:

Prep:30 mins Cook:3 hrs 15 mins Total:3 hrs 45 mins
Servings:16 Yield:

1. Preheat the smoker for high temperature. If you are using a charcoal grill, use about twice the normal amount of charcoal. Soak wood chips in a pan of water, and set them next to the grill.
2. Discard neck and giblets from turkey. Rinse the bird and pat dry. Putin a large disposable roasting pan.
3. In a medium bowl, whisk together sage, ground black pepper, celery salt, basil, and vegetable oil. Drain the mixture evenly over the turkey. Turn the turkey breast side down in the pan, and cover loosely with aluminum foil.
4. Place the roasting pan on the preheated grill. Throw a handful of the wood chips onto the coals. Close the lid, and cook for 1 hour.

5. Throw about 2 more handfuls of soaked wood chips on the fire. Sprinkle 1/2 the honey over the bird, and replace the foil. Close the lid of the grill, and continue cooking for 1 1/2 to 2 hours, or until internal temperature reaches 180 degrees F (80 degrees C) in the thickest part of the thigh.
6. Open turkey, and carefully turn it breast side up in the roasting pan. Baste with remaining honey. Leave the turkey uncovered, and cook for 15 minutes. The cooked honey will be very dark.

Nutrition Facts:

- Calories;
- Protein 68.9g;
- Carbohydrates 25.3g;
- Fat 28.8g;
- Cholesterol 228.5mg;
- Sodium 776.3mg.

23. Smoked Salmon Sushi Roll

Ingredients:

- 2 cups Japanese sushi rice
- 6 tablespoons rice wine vinegar
- 6 sheets nori (dry seaweed)
- 1 avocado - peeled, pitted, and sliced
- 1 cucumber, peeled and sliced
- 8 ounces smoked salmon, cut into long strips
- 2 tablespoons wasabi paste

Preparation:

Prep:30 mins Additional: 4 hrs 30 mins Total:5 hrsServings:6Yield: 6 rolls

1. Dry rice for 4 hours. Drain the rice and cook in a rice cooker with 2 cups of water. Rice must be slightly dry as vinegar will be added later.
2. Immediately after the rice is made, mix 6 tablespoons of rice vinegar into the hot rice. Spread rice on a plate until completely cool.
3. Put 1 sheet of seaweed on a bamboo mat, roll a thin layer of cool rice on the seaweed. Leave at least 1/2 inch top and bottom edge of the seaweed uncovered. This is for easier sealing later. Dot some wasabi on the rice. Prepare cucumber, avocado, and smoked salmon to the rice. Position them about 1 inch away from the bottom edge of the seaweed.
4. Slightly moisten the top edge of the seaweed. Roll from bottom to the top edge with the help of the bamboo mat tightly. Slice roll into 8 equal pieces and serve. Repeat for other rolls.

Nutrition Facts:

- 291 calories;
- Protein 11.1g;
- Carbohydrates 45.1g;
- Fat 6.9g;
- Cholesterol 8.7mg;
- Sodium 404.7mg.

24. Salmon Wraps

Ingredients:

- 1 (8 ounces) package cream cheese, softened
- 2 tablespoons chopped fresh dill
- 2 tablespoons chopped fresh chives
- 1 tablespoon lemon juice
- 3 (8 inches) flour tortillas
- 6 slices smoked salmon

Preparation:

Prep time:10 mins, Total:10 mins, Servings:24, Yield:24 servings

1. Combine cream cheese, dill, chives, and lemon juice together in a bowl.
2. Smear cream cheese on 1/3 of each tortilla. Lay 2 salmon slices on top; roll tightly and seal ends with a dab of cream cheese. Cut each roll into 1-inch parts.

Nutrition facts:

- 61 calories
- Protein 2.5g
- Carbohydrates 3.7g
- Fat 4g
- Cholesterol 11.9mg
- Sodium 112mg

25. Smoked Prime Rib Roast

Ingredients:

- Original recipe yields 10 servings
- Ingredient Checklist
- 2 ½ teaspoons kosher salt
- 1 (5 pounds) prime rib roast, bones removed
- 5 tablespoons olive oil
- 2 tablespoons cracked black pepper
- 2 teaspoons garlic powder
- 2 teaspoons dried rosemary
- 2 teaspoons dried thyme
- 1 teaspoon onion powder
- 1 teaspoon paprika
- ½ teaspoon cayenne pepper

Preparation:

Prep:10 minsCook:3 hrs 15 minsAdditional:6 hrs 15 minsTotal:9 hrs 40 minsServings:10Yield:10 servings

1. Spray salt over the entire roast and wrap with plastic wrap. Freeze, 4 hours to 24 hours.
2. Mix olive oil, black pepper, garlic powder, rosemary, thyme, onion powder, paprika, and cayenne pepper together in a bowl. Set aside for flavors to blend, at least 1 hour.
3. Pour most of the oil mixture over the roast and massage into the top and sides of the meat. Flip the roast and pour the remaining oil mixture over the roast and massage. Place roast on a plate and refrigerate, 1 hour to 12 hours.

4. Preheat the smoker to 225 degrees F to 230 degrees F. Add hickory or pecan wood chips to the smoker.
5. Enter a meat thermometer into the thickest part of the roast. Put roast into the smoker and roast until internal heat reaches 145 degrees F (63 degrees C), 3 to 3 1/2 hours.
6. Preheat a smoker to 500 degrees F to 550 degrees F.
7. Bake the roast in the preheated smoker until the crust is crunchy, producing a reverse sear, 15 to 20 minutes. Allow roast to rest 10 to 15 minutes before slicing.

Nutrition facts:

- 358 calories
- Protein 27.3g
- Carbohydrates 1.9g
- Fat 26.2g
- Cholesterol 80.4mg
- Sodium 554.7mg

26. Smoked Salmon Pasta Salad

Ingredients:

- 11 ounces multi-colored fusilli pasta
- 1 small carrot, grated
- 1 small onion, chopped
- ½ cup diced cucumber
- ½ cup diced celery
- 8 ounces smoked salmon, cut into 3/4 inch pieces
- ⅓ cup mayonnaise
- 2 teaspoons lemon juice
- 1 pinch salt
- 1 pinch ground black pepper
- 1 pinch cayenne pepper

Preparation:

Prep:15 minsCook:15 mins Total:30 mins Servings:6
Yield:6 servings

1. Stuff a large pot with lightly salted water and bring to a rolling boil over high heat. Stir in the fusilli; revert to a boil. Cook the pasta until the pasta has cooked through, but is still firm to the bite, about 12 minutes. Drain well and rinse with cold water. Transfer cooled pasta to a large bowl.
2. Stir the carrot, onion, cucumber, celery, and salmon with the pasta; mix well.
3. Mix the mayonnaise, lemon juice, salt, pepper, and cayenne pepper in a small bowl; mix well. Drain sauce over pasta mixture. Mix well to cover evenly.

Nutrition Facts:

- 328 calories
- Protein 14.2g
- Carbohydrates 40.6g
- Fat 12.6g
- Cholesterol 13.3mg
- Sodium 383.2mg

27. Basic Brine for Smoking Meat

Ingredients:

- ¼ cup kosher salt
- ¼ cup packed brown sugar
- 4 cups water

Preparation:

Prep:10 min, Total:10 mins Servings:8 Yield:1 quart

1. In a medium bowl, combine the salt, sugar, and water. Whisk vigorously until all the salt and sugar are dissolved. Then drain this mixture over the meat, poultry, or fish that you are preparing. Soak for several hours, or overnight.
2. Make certain the meat is fully immersed in the brine, and make more brine as needed to fully cover the meat.

Nutrition facts:

- 26 calories
- Protein 0g
- Carbohydrates 6.7g
- Fat 0g
- Cholesterol 0mg
- Sodium 2852.1mg

28. Salty and Sweet Cranberry Citrus Brine

Ingredients:

- 1 cup kosher salt
- 1 (12 fluid ounce) can freeze orange juice concentrate
- 1 (12 fluid ounce) can freeze cranberry juice concentrate
- 1-gallon water
- ½ cup brown sugar
- 1 cinnamon stick
- 1 lemon, cut into wedges
- 1 orange, cut into wedges
- 1 red onion, cut into wedges
- 3 cloves garlic
- 4 bay leaves
- 1 tablespoon dried thyme leaves
- 1 tablespoon freshly ground black pepper

Preparation:

Prep:10 mins, Total: 10 mins, Servings:12 Yield:6 cups of brine

1. In a large stockpot, whisk together the kosher salt, orange juice concentrate, cranberry juice concentrate, water, brown sugar, cinnamon stick, lemon wedges, orange wedges, onion wedges, garlic cloves, bay leaves, thyme, and black pepper; stir till the salt and brown sugar have dissolved. To use, put a whole turkey into the

brine, cover, and refrigerate 14 to 16 hours before roasting. Cut used brine.

Nutrition facts:

- 156 calories
- Protein 0.8g
- Carbohydrates 39.2g
- Fat 0.1g
- Cholesterol 0mg
- Sodium 7605.8mg

29. Turkey Brine

Ingredients:

- 2 gallons
- 1 gallon vegetable broth
- 1 cup sea salt
- 1 tablespoon crushed dried rosemary
- 1 tablespoon dried sage
- 1 tablespoon dried thyme
- 1 tablespoon dried savory
- 1-gallon ice water

Preparation:

Prep: 5 mins Cook:15 mins Additional:8 hrs Total:8 hrs 20 mins Servings:15Yield:

1. In a large stockpot, mix the vegetable broth, sea salt, rosemary, sage, thyme, and savory. Bring to a boil, stirring constantly to be sure salt is dissolved. Transfer from heat, and let cool to room temperature.
2. When the broth mixture is cool, pour it into a clean 5-gallon bucket. Stir in the ice water.
3. Clean and dry your turkey. Make sure you have removed the innards. Put the turkey, breast down, into the brine. Make sure that the cavity gets filled. Place the bucket in the refrigerator overnight.
4. Remove the turkey carefully draining off the excess brine and pat dry. Discard excess brine.
5. Sear the turkey as desired, reserving the drippings for gravy. Keep in mind that brined turkeys cook

20 to 30 minutes faster so watch the temperature gauge.

Nutrition facts:

- 3 calories;
- Protein 0.1g;
- Carbohydrates 0.6g;
- Fat 0.1g;
- Cholesterol 0mg;
- Sodium 5640.3mg

30. Smoked Eggs

Ingredients:

- 6 fresh raw eggs in the shell
- Salt and ground black pepper to taste

Preparation:

Prep:5 min Cook:2 hrs Total 2 hrs 5 mins

1. Preheat a smoker grill to 225 degrees F (110 degrees C). Add wood chips.
2. Place whole eggs directly on the grill of the preheated smoker. Cook, without turning, for 2 hours, maintaining an even temperature.
3. Transfer eggs to a plate and let them cool completely before peeling. Season with salt and pepper.

Nutrition facts:

- 63 calories
- Protein 5.5g
- Carbohydrates 0.3g
- Fat 4.4g
- Cholesterol 163.7mg
- Sodium 87.4mg

31. Smoked Chicken Hot Wings

Ingredients:

- 1 tablespoon kosher salt
- 1 ½ teaspoon ground black pepper
- 1 ½ teaspoon Cajun seasoning
- 2 ½ pounds chicken wings
- Sauce:
- ⅔ cup hot pepper sauce (such as Frank's RedHot®)
- ½ cup butter
- 1 ½ tablespoon white vinegar
- ½ teaspoon Worcestershire sauce
- ⅛ teaspoon garlic powder
- 1 pinch salt to taste

Preparation:

Prep:15 minsCook:1 hr 8 minsTotal:1 hr 23 mins

1. Heat a smoker to 225 degrees F according to.
2. Whisk 1 tablespoon salt, pepper, and Cajun seasoning in a small bowl to make dry rub. Spray over chicken wings.
3. Sear chicken wings in the preheated smoker until tender, 1 to 1 1/4 hour.
4. Mix hot pepper sauce, butter, vinegar, Worcestershire sauce, garlic powder, and salt in a small saucepan over low heat. Cook, stirring often until butter is melted and sauce is smooth. Remove from heat.
5. Preheat the smoker grill for medium-high heat and lightly oil the grate.

6. Transfer smoked wings to a large bowl; stir in 1/2 of the sauce until wings are evenly coated.
7. Grill coated wings until skin is browned and starting to get crispy, 4 to 5 minutes per side. Transfer to a large bowl and stir in the remaining sauce until wings are well-coated.

Nutrition Facts:

- 209 calories
- Protein 9.8g
- Carbohydrates 0.9g
- Fat 18.5g
- Cholesterol 60.2mg
- Sodium 1435.4mg

32. Easy Grilled Chicken Wings

Ingredients:

- 20 chicken wings
- 20 chicken wings
- 2 tablespoons olive oil, or more as needed
- 3 teaspoons garlic salt
- 3 teaspoons ground black pepper

Preparation:

Prep:10 mins Cook:30 mins Total:40 mins
Servings:20Yield:

1. Preheat smoker grill for high temperature and lightly oil the grate.
2. Tuck in the chicken wing flaps so the wing forms a triangle.
3. Mix olive oil with some of the garlic salt and pepper in a large bowl. Add a few chicken wings and turn to coat with seasonings. Add more wings, remaining garlic salt, and remaining pepper and turn to coat. Repeat until all wings are coated. Put on the preheated grill.
4. Grill till the wings are well browned, tender, and no longer pink at the bone and juices run clear, turning some times and rearranging them so they cook evenly 30 to 40 minutes.

Nutrition Facts:

- 80 calories
- Protein 6.2g
- Carbohydrates 0.3g
- Fat 5.8g
- Cholesterol 19.3mg
- Sodium 290.8mg

33. Smoked Chicken Wings

Ingredients:

- 16 chicken wings, tips discarded
- ¼ cup olive oil
- ¼ cup dry rub for chicken (such as McCormick® Grill Mates®)
- 1 pound mesquite wood chips, soaked in water
- 1 (8 ounces) bottle blue cheese salad dressing

Preparation:

Prep:10 minsCook:2 hrsTotal:2 hrs 10 minsServings:8Yield:16 wings

1. Put chicken wings in a large bowl. Pour in olive oil; toss with hands until coated. Coat wings evenly with dry rub.
2. Light charcoal and heat smoker to 170 to 200 degrees F according to manufacturer's instructions.
3. Remove wood chips and place half of them directly on the charcoal. Spread wings evenly on the cooking grate skin-side down.
4. Smoke wings until fragrant, about 1 hour.
5. Flip wings. Add remaining wood chips to the charcoal. Continue smoking until an instant-read thermometer inserted near the bone reads 165 degrees F, about 1 hour more.
6. Serve chicken wings with blue cheese dressing.

Nutrition Facts:

- 295 calories
- Protein 14.2g
- Carbohydrates 3.7g
- Fat 25g
- Cholesterol 38.9mg
- Sodium 1075.9mg

34. Easy Smoked Sausage Skillet

Ingredients:

- 1 (14 ounce) package Hillshire Farm® Smoked Sausage, diagonally cut into 1/4-inch slices
- ¼ cup olive oil
- 2 cloves garlic, crushed
- 1 large red bell pepper, sliced thin
- 1 small yellow onion, sliced thin
- 1 (10 ounce) package frozen broccoli, thawed
- ½ cup chicken broth or water
- ½ cup tomato sauce
- 2 cups instant rice
- ½ cup shredded mozzarella cheese

Preparation:

Additional:20 minsTotal:20 minsServings:4Yield:4 servings

1. Heat olive oil and crushed garlic, mix in smoked sausage slices and cook until smoked sausage is browned.
2. Add pepper, onion, broccoli, chicken broth and tomato sauce and cook for about 10 minutes until vegetables are tender and the liquid is absorbed.
3. In the meantime, cook rice according to package instructions. Stir rice into the skillet, spray with cheese and serve.

Nutrition Facts:

- 722 calories
- Protein 22.8g
- Carbohydrates 54.6g
- Fat 45g
- Cholesterol 71.7mg
- Sodium 1243.1mg

35. Cheesy Smoked Sausage and Rice Skillet

Ingredients:

- 1 yellow onion, chopped
- 1 (4 ounce) can sliced mushrooms, drained
- 1 red bell pepper, cut into 1/2-inch strips
- 1 cup frozen peas
- 3 cups cooked long grain white rice
- 1 (10.75 ounce) can condensed broccoli cheese soup
- ¼ cup milk

Preparation:

Prep:10 mins Cook: 20 mins Total:30 mins

1. Slice sausage on an angle into 1/2-inch slices.
2. Warm a large skillet over medium heat for 2 minutes; add sausage, onions and peppers. Sear, stirring frequently 5-6 minutes or until sausage is lightly browned and vegetables are tender. Add peas and cook 3-4 minutes, stirring occasionally until peas are hot.
3. Lightly stir in cooked rice, soup, milk and mushrooms if desired; heat through.

Nutrition Facts:

- 421 calories
- Protein 14.3g
- Carbohydrates 43.7g
- Fat 20.7g
- Cholesterol 50.6mg
- Sodium 1019.9mg

36. Smoked Sausage, White Bean and Spinach Pasta

Ingredients:

- 1 (14 ounce) package Hillshire Farm® Smoked Sausage, diagonally cut into 1/4-inch slices
- 2 teaspoons olive oil
- 6 ounces bow tie pasta, cooked and drained
- 1 (15 ounce) can white beans, rinsed and drained
- 1 medium zucchini, sliced into thin rounds
- ½ cup vegetable broth
- ½ pint cherry tomatoes, halved
- 1 (6 ounce) package fresh spinach
- ¼ cup toasted pine nuts

Preparation:

Additional:15 minsTotal:15 mins Servings:4Yield:4 servings

1. Sear pasta according to package directions. Drain and set aside.
2. Heat a dry large skillet over medium-low heat and toast pine nuts, stirring frequently, until pine nuts are golden in spots, about 3 minutes. Transfer and set aside.
3. Heat 2 teaspoons olive oil in the same skillet on medium-high heat. Saute the smoked sausage for 5 minutes, or till the golden brown, stirring occasionally. Remove smoked sausage and set aside.
4. Add the zucchini and vegetable broth to the skillet and simmer until zucchini are soft, about 5

minutes. Combine spinach, white beans and cherry tomatoes; continue to simmer for 2 minutes until spinach is wilted and tomatoes are soft.

5. Turn the heat to low; add the pasta and smoked sausage to the vegetables mixing well to blend and cook for 30 seconds until heated through.

6. Garnish with toasted pine nuts and serve hot.

Nutrition Facts:

- 666 calories
- Protein 26.3g
- Carbohydrates 57.2g
- Fat 36.8g
- Cholesterol 62mg
- Sodium 1170.5mg

37. Smoked Sausage White Bean Chili

Ingredients:

- 1 (14 ounce) package Hillshire Farm® Smoked Sausage, cut into 1/2-inch cubes
- 1 cup chicken broth
- 2 (15.8 ounce) cans great Northern beans, drained, rinsed
- 1 (4.5 ounce) can chopped green chilies, drained
- 2 teaspoons chili powder
- 1 teaspoon ground cumin

Preparation:

Prep:5 mins Cook:15 mins Total:20 mins Servings:6 Yield:6 servings

1. Brown sausage in 4-quart saucepan over medium-high heat for 5 minutes. Add broth; stir to combine any browned bits on the bottom of pan.
2. Add remaining ingredients. Bring to boil; reduce heat, cook uncovered for 10 minutes, stirring occasionally.

Nutrition Facts:

- 406 calories
- Protein 19.8g
- Carbohydrates 36.8g
- Fat 19.8g
- Cholesterol 42.2mg
- Sodium 992.7mg

38. Smoked Sausage Gnocchi with Sun-Dried Tomatoes

Ingredients:

- 1 pound gnocchi
- 1 (14 ounce) package Hillshire Farm® Smoked Sausage, cut into 1/2-inch slices
- ¼ cup julienned sun-dried tomatoes in oil
- 2 cloves garlic, minced
- 4 cups baby spinach
- ½ cup shredded Parmesan cheese

Preparation:

Prep:3 mins Cook:12 minsTotal:15 mins
Servings:6Yield:6 servings

1. Make gnocchi according to directions; drain and keep warm.
2. Sear and stir sausage, garlic and sun-dried tomatoes in oil a large skillet over medium-high heat 5 minutes or until sausage is lightly browned.

Beat in spinach; stir gently until spinach wilts. Stir in gnocchi; heat through. Spray with Parmesan cheese; serve immediately.

Nutrition Facts:

- 377 calories
- Protein 13.6g
- Carbohydrates 19.3g
- Fat 26.8g
- Cholesterol 61.4mg
- Sodium 753.9mg

39. Smoked Sausage and Tuscan White Bean Soup

Ingredients:

- 1 pound dried great Northern beans, rinsed and sorted
- 6 cups water
- 1 tablespoon olive oil
- 1 (12 ounce) package Hillshire Farm® Rope Smoked Sausage, halved lengthwise and cut into 1/2" half-moons
- 1 ½ cups chopped yellow onions
- 2 tablespoons minced garlic
- 1 tablespoon chopped fresh thyme
- 8 cups unsalted chicken stock
- 2 teaspoons kosher salt
- 5 cups thinly sliced kale
- 4 ounces uncooked small shell pasta
- 1 teaspoon lemon zest
- ½ teaspoon crushed red pepper
- 1 (14.5 ounce) can diced tomatoes, drained
- ½ cup grated Parmesan cheese

Preparation:

Prep:20 mins Cook:55 mins Additional:15 mins Total:1 hr 30 mins Servings:6 Yield:6 servings

1. Place the programmable pressure cooker to Saute. Add rinsed and drained beans and 6 cups water. Bring to a boil and fasten and lock the lid. Switch cooker to high pressure for 1 minute. Release

pressure manually and carefully drain beans. Transfer beans to a bowl, and set aside.
2. Add oil and sausage; cook 7 to 8 minutes, stirring seldom, until sausage begins to brown. whisk onions, garlic, and thyme; cook 4 to 5 minutes, stirring occasionally, until onions are translucent. Add beans, stock, and salt. Close the pressure cooker and fasten lid. Lock and seal steam valve. Set to high pressure and cook until beans are tender, 10 minutes. Release pressure manually.
3. Uncover pressure cooker. Stir in kale, pasta, zest, crushed red pepper, and tomatoes. Fasten and lock lid, set cooker to HIGH PRESSURE and cook for 5 minutes. Release pressure manually. Serve in bowls.

Nutrition Facts:

- 643 calories
- Protein 37g
- Carbohydrates 78.3g
- Fat 21.9g
- Cholesterol 40.9mg
- Sodium 1576.5mg

40. Multi-Cooker Chili with Hillshire Farm® Smoked Sausage

Ingredients:

- 1 cup dried pinto beans
- 1 cup dried black beans
- 1 tablespoon olive oil
- 1 (14 ounce) package Hillshire Farm® Smoked Sausage, cut crosswise into 1/2-inch-thick slices
- 1 cup diced yellow onion
- 1 cup diced green bell pepper
- 4 garlic cloves, minced
- 1 teaspoon kosher salt
- 1 (1.25 ounce) package chili seasoning mix
- 1 (14.5 ounce) can diced fire-roasted tomatoes
- 3 cups chicken stock

Preparation:

Prep:20 mins Cook:40 mins Additional 8 hrs 15 mins Total:9 hrs 15 mins Servings:8Yield:8 cups

1. Put the beans in a large mixing bowl and add 6 cups of water. Let rest for 8 to 12 hours. Drain.
2. Using the Saute function, warm the multi-cooker over high heat. Add the olive oil then smoked sausage and cook, stirring occasionally, for 5 to 6 minutes, until lightly browned and some of the fat has rendered. Remove with a slotted spoon to a plate.
3. Add onion, bell pepper, and garlic. Cook for 3 minutes, stirring occasionally. Add the salt, chili seasoning, beans, diced tomatoes, and chicken

stock. Stir well to mix, scraping browned bits from the bottom of the pot.
4. Lock the lid in place and turn the top lid to seal. Set the multi-cooker to cook at high pressure for 20 minutes. let 10 to 15 minutes for pressure to build. Allow pressure release naturally for 15 minutes, then release remaining pressure manually.
5. Return the sausage to the pot and stir well to combine.

Nutrition Facts:

- 339 calories
- Protein 15.1g
- Carbohydrates 31.7g
- Fat 16.9g
- Cholesterol 31.3mg
- Sodium 1480.6mg

41. Hawaiian Pineapple Sweet & Sour Smoked Sausage

Ingredients:

- 1 (14 ounce) package Hillshire Farm® Smoked Sausage, cut into 1/2-inch slices
- 1 red bell pepper, seeded, chopped
- ¼ cup sweet chili garlic sauce*
- 1 cup fresh pineapple, cut into 1/2-inch pieces
- 3 cups cooked rice

Preparation:

 Prep:3 mins Cook:12 minsTotal:15 mins Servings:6 Yield:6 servings

1. Sear and stir sausage and bell peppers over medium-high heat for 5 minutes or until sausage is lightly browned and peppers are tender.
2. Mix chili garlic sauce and pineapple; cook and stir for 5 minutes.
3. Serve over cooked rice.

Nutrition Facts:

- Per Serving
- 364 calories
- Protein 10.7g
- Carbohydrates 34.9g
- Fat 19.3g
- Cholesterol 41.3mg
- Sodium 681.2mg

42. Hillshire Farm® Smoked Sausage and Squash Boats

Ingredients:

- 2 (1 pound) acorn squash
- 4 tablespoons water
- 1 (14 ounce) package Hillshire Farm® Smoked Sausage, halved lengthwise and cut crosswise into 1/2-inch pieces
- ½ (8.8 ounce) package cooked whole grain brown rice
- ¾ cup finely shredded Parmesan cheese, divided
- 2 teaspoons snipped fresh sage
- 1 teaspoon snipped fresh thyme
- ¼ teaspoon ground black pepper
- 1 tablespoon balsamic vinegar

Preparation:

Prep:20 minsCook:20 mins Total:40 minsServings:4Yield:4 squash boats

1. Slice squash in half lengthwise; discard seeds and strings.
2. In a 2-quart baking dish, prepare two squash halves, cut sides down; add in 2 tablespoons of the water. Wrap with vented plastic wrap. Microwave 7 to 10 minutes or until squash is just tender; keep warm. Repeat with the remaining squash halves.
3. Meanwhile, in a large skillet, cook sausage over medium-high heat for 6 minutes or until browned,

adding rice, 1/2 cup of the cheese, sage, thyme, and black pepper in the last 2 minutes of cooking.
4. To serve, fill squash halves with sausage mixture. Spray with remaining 1/4 cup cheese and drizzle with balsamic vinegar.

Nutrition Facts:

- 528 calories;
- Protein 20.8g;
- Carbohydrates 37.4g;
- Fat 33g;
- Cholesterol 72.8mg;
- Sodium 1114.8mg.

43. Sheet Pan Pizza with Hillshire Farm Smoked Sausage & Burst Cherry Tomatoes

Ingredients:

- 1 (16 ounce) package frozen pizza crust
- 6 tablespoons olive oil, divided
- 1 tablespoon chopped fresh garlic
- 1 tablespoon chopped fresh oregano
- 1 (8 ounce) ball fresh mozzarella, thinly sliced
- 1 cup shredded low-moisture mozzarella cheese
- ½ cup thinly sliced yellow bell pepper
- ¼ cup thinly sliced red onion
- 1 (14 ounce) package Hillshire Farm® Smoked Sausage, cut crosswise into 1/2-inch-thick slices
- ⅔ cup cherry tomatoes, halved

Preparation:

Prep:30 mins Cook:20 mins Additional:5 mins Total:55 mins

1. Thaw and let pizza crust rise according to package directions.
2. Spread 3 tablespoons oil over the base of an 11x17-inch sheet tray. Stretch the dough to meet all corners and edges of the sheet tray. If the dough is difficult to stretch, let rest for 10 minutes, then begin to stretch again.
3. Preheat the smoker to 450 degrees F. In a small bowl, mix together the remaining 3 tablespoons oil, chopped garlic, and fresh oregano. Drizzle evenly and spread over the top of the crust.

4. Top with fresh mozzarella slices, then shredded mozzarella, yellow bell pepper, red onion, smoked sausage slices, and cherry tomatoes.
5. Place on the bottom rack of the oven. Bake for 18 to 20 minutes, until the crust is golden. Let cool for 5 minutes, then serve.

Nutrition Facts:

- 706 calories
- Protein 26.5g
- Carbohydrates 42.5g
- Fat 46.2g
- Cholesterol 83.1mg
- Sodium 1237.7mg

44. Creamy Pasta Toss with Smoked Sausage

Ingredients:

- 1 (8 ounce) package uncooked pappardelle pasta
- 1 tablespoon olive oil
- 1 (12 ounce) package Hillshire Farm® Rope Smoked Sausage, cut into 1/2" coins
- 1 (8 ounce) package sliced cremini mushrooms
- 2 tablespoons unsalted butter
- 6 cloves garlic, thinly sliced
- 1 ¼ cups half-and-half
- 1 (4 ounce) package cream cheese
- 1 cup shredded Parmesan cheese, divided
- ½ teaspoon kosher salt
- ½ teaspoon black pepper
- ½ cup refrigerated prepared pesto
- ⅓ cup thinly sliced basil

Preparation:

Prep:10 mins Cook:20 mins Total:30 mins

1. Sear pasta, drain, reserving 1/2 cup pasta cooking water.
2. Warmth oil in a large high-sided skillet over medium-high. Add sausage and mushrooms and cook about 6 minutes, stirring occasionally, until browned. Transfer to a plate; carefully wipe pan clean as it may be hot.
3. Melt butter in pan over medium; add garlic and cook until it just begins to brown, stirring occasionally, 2 to 3 minutes. Add half-and-half and

cream cheese; bring to a simmer, whisking constantly until smooth. Shift from heat and stir in 3/4 cup Parmesan cheese, salt, and pepper until smooth. Put pasta and sausage mixture; toss to coat. Thin sauce with reserved pasta water if necessary.
4. Serve in shallow bowls topped with pesto, basil, and remaining 1/4 cup cheese.

Nutrition Facts:

- 1023 calories
- Protein 38.4g
- Carbohydrates 56.8g
- Fat 72.5g
- Cholesterol 154.4mg
- Sodium 1690.3mg

45. Linguine with Hillshire Farm® Smoked Sausage and Greens

Ingredients:

- 4 egg yolks
- ½ cup whole milk
- ½ cup freshly grated Parmesan cheese
- 2 teaspoons lemon zest
- ¼ teaspoon freshly ground black pepper
- 8 ounces dried linguine
- 1 (14 ounces) package Hillshire Farm® Smoked Sausage, bias-sliced 1/2-inch thick
- 1 clove garlic, minced
- 2 cups coarsely chopped spinach
- ¼ cup fresh Italian parsley leaves
- 1 teaspoon Freshly grated Parmesan cheese

Preparation:

Prep:30 mins Cook:20 mins Total:50 mins

1. In a medium bowl, mix together egg yolks, milk, 1/2 cup cheese, lemon zest, and black pepper. Set aside.
2. In a 4-quart Dutch smoker, cook linguine in a large quantity of boiling salted water according to package directions, about 11 minutes. Drain, reserving 1/4 cup of the cooking water. Return linguine to the smoker.
3. Meanwhile, in a large skillet, sear sausage over medium heat for 5 minutes or until browned, adding garlic in the last minute of cooking.
4. Drain egg yolk mixture over linguine in the smoker. Add sausage and spinach; toss to coat. The heat from the pan and the linguine cooks and thickens the egg yolk, making a silky sauce. stir in enough reserved pasta cooking water to reach desired consistency. Toss with parsley.
5. Serve immediately. Spray with additional Parmesan cheese, if desired.

Nutrition Facts:

- 663 calories
- Protein 28.4g
- Carbohydrates 50.1g
- Fat 38.2g
- Cholesterol 279.2mg
- Sodium 1056.6mg

46. Smoked Sausage and Butternut Squash Pasta

Ingredients:

- Ingredient Checklist
- 8 ounces uncooked rigatoni pasta
- 8 ounces Hillshire Farm® Rope Smoked Sausage, cut into bias-cut pieces
- 4 cups chopped butternut squash
- 1 tablespoon olive oil
- 6 tablespoons unsalted butter, divided
- ¼ cup fresh sage leaves, chopped
- 3 tablespoons fresh lemon juice
- 1 cup grated Parmesan cheese
- ½ teaspoon kosher salt
- ½ teaspoon black pepper

Preparation:

Prep:10 mins Cook:30 mins Total:40 mins Servings:4
Yield:8 cups

1. Sear pasta according to package directions; drain.
2. Preheat the oven to 450 degrees F. put sausage and squash on a large baking pan. Drizzle with oil; toss to coat.
3. Roast in a preheated smoker for 12 minutes. Roll with 3 tablespoons cubed butter and sage; return to the oven for 12-14 minutes, until squash is caramelized and tender.
4. Melt remaining butter in a large skillet over medium heat. Toss in pasta, sausage mixture, lemon juice, 3/4 cup of the cheese, salt, and

pepper. Serve in shallow bowls topped with remaining 1/4 cup cheese.

Nutrition Facts:

- 721 calories
- Protein 24g
- Carbohydrates 62.5g
- Fat 44.1g
- Cholesterol 98.8mg
- Sodium 1073.4mg

47. Smoked Sausage with Potatoes, Sauerkraut & Ale

Ingredients:

- 1 (14 ounces) package Hillshire Farm® Smoked Sausage, diagonally cut into 1/4-inch slices
- 2 tablespoons vegetable oil
- 2 cups potatoes, diced into 1-inch pieces
- 12 fluid ounces your favorite ale
- 1 cup sauerkraut, rinsed and drained
- 2 tablespoons whole-grain mustard

Preparation:

Prep:5 mins Cook:15 mins Total:20 mins Servings:6 Yield:6 servings

1. Sear sausage in a large skillet over medium-high heat for 3 minutes, turning occasionally. Remove sausage and set aside.
2. Mix oil and potatoes to the skillet and cook until golden brown.
3. Add ale, sauerkraut, and mustard to skillet, mixing with potatoes until blended. Cook over medium-high heat for 2 minutes.
4. Turn the sausage to the skillet, continue cooking for 10 minutes or until potatoes are tender.

Nutrition Facts:

- 343 calories
- Protein 9.7g
- Carbohydrates 17g
- Fat 23.5g
- Cholesterol 41.3m
- Sodium 785.2mg

48. Cheesy Potatoes with Smoked Sausage

Ingredients:

- 1 (1 pound) package Hillshire Farm® Smoked Sausage
- 1 (20 ounce) package refrigerated shredded hash brown potatoes
- 2 cups shredded Cheddar cheese
- 1 cup sour cream
- 1 medium onion, chopped
- ¼ cup butter or margarine, melted
- ¼ teaspoon ground black pepper

Preparation:

Prep:10 min Cook 45 minsTotal:55 mins

1. Preheat the smoker to 350 degrees F. Gently spray a 13 x 9-inch baking pan with non-stick cooking spray. Slice sausage into 1/2" cubes. Mix all ingredients in a large bowl.
2. Spread mixture equally in the ready pan. Bake 40-45 minutes or until lightly browned. Let stay 5 minutes before serving.

Nutrition Facts:

- 647 calories
- Protein 21.5g
- Carbohydrates 26.6g
- Fat 49.8g
- Cholesterol 124mg
- Sodium 1021.6mg

49. Smoked Sausage and Orzo Stuffed Peppers

Ingredients:

- 1 tablespoon olive oil
- 1 (14 ounces) package Hillshire Farm® Smoked Sausage, cut into 1/4-inch-wide half-moons
- 1 medium onion, 1/2-inch dice
- 1 clove garlic, minced
- 1 tablespoon Italian seasoning
- 1 tablespoon white wine vinegar
- 2 cups orzo pasta, cooked according to package directions
- ½ teaspoon salt
- ½ teaspoon pepper
- ½ cup shredded mozzarella cheese
- 1 ¾ cups marinara sauce
- ¼ teaspoon ground cinnamon
- 6 bell peppers

Preparation:

Prep:15 mins Cook:25 mins Total:40 mins
Servings:6Yield:6 servings

1. Heat smoker to 400 degrees F.
2. Heat oil in a large skillet over medium heat. Add smoked sausage, onion, garlic, and Italian seasoning and cook for 6-9 minutes, stirring occasionally, until onions are soft and smoked sausage is brown. Stir in white wine vinegar, cooked orzo, salt, pepper, and 1/4 cup mozzarella; transfer from heat and set aside.

3. Whisk together the marinara sauce and cinnamon and stir 1/4 cup of the sauce into the skillet. Spoon remaining sauce into the bottom of a 9x9-inch baking dish.
4. Slice the tops off of the peppers, remove the seeds, stuff them with the orzo-smoked sausage mixture, and place them in a baking dish. Sprinkle with remaining mozzarella cheese and bake until heated through 25 minutes.

Nutrition Facts:

- 609 calories
- Protein 22.3g
- Carbohydrates 71.6g
- Fat 25.9g
- Cholesterol 48.8mg
- Sodium 1126.2mg

50. Smoked Sausage Pizza Pasta Skillet

Ingredients:

- 2 tablespoons olive oil
- 1 (10 ounces) package button mushrooms, quartered
- 1 (14 ounces) package Hillshire Farm® Smoked Sausage, diagonally cut into 1/4-inch slices
- ½ cup pepperoni slices, cut into halves
- 1 teaspoon Italian seasoning
- ½ teaspoon salt
- 1 (16 ounces) package whole wheat penne pasta, cooked according to package directions
- 2 cups marinara sauce
- 1 cup shredded mozzarella cheese

Preparation:

Additional:17 minsTotal:17 minsServings:6Yield:6 servings

1. Heat oven broiler.
2. Heat a large oven-safe 10-inch skillet over medium heat. Add oil, mushrooms and smoked sausage; cook about 5 minutes until mushrooms are soft and smoked sausage is browned.
3. Add pepperoni, Italian seasoning and salt and cook for 2 minutes. Stir in cooked pasta and marinara sauce. Sprinkle with mozzarella and place under the broiler just until cheese is melted and starting to bubble. Sprinkle with extra Italian seasoning to serve.

Nutrition Facts

- 624 calories
- Protein 26.8g
- Carbohydrates 42.9g
- Fat 37.8g
- Cholesterol 74.9mg
- Sodium 1551.1mg

51. Barbecue Smoked Sausage Pizza

Ingredients

- 1 (12 ounces) package Hillshire Farm Beef Smoked Sausage
- 2 (14 ounce) packages 12-inch size Italian pizza crust
- ⅔ cup prepared barbecue sauce
- 1 cup thinly sliced red onion
- 1 green bell pepper, seeded, cut into thin strips
- 2 cups shredded mozzarella cheese

Preparation:

Prep: 20 mins, Cook: 20 mins, Total: 40 mins, Servings: 8, Yield: 16 slices

1. Preheat the smoker to 425 degrees F. Sliced sausage on an angle in 1/4-inch slices. Put crusts on 2 baking sheets; spread 1/3 cup barbecue sauce on each crust.
2. Top each pizza with 1/2 each of sausage, red onion, pepper, and mozzarella cheese.
3. Bake for 20 minutes or until the crust is crispy and cheese is lightly browned. Cut each pizza into 8 slices.

Nutrition Facts:

- 541 calories
- Protein 26.5g
- Carbohydrates 62.7g
- Fat 22g
- Cholesterol 54.7mg
- Sodium 1383.9mg